Teaching For Money by Glenn R Clarke

Introduction:
"Profitable Pursuits: Unleashing Your Passion for Financial Freedom"

Chapter 1:
"Teaching as a Passion: Turning Knowledge into Profit"

Chapter 2:
"My Journey into becoming self-employed: Triumph Over Adversity"

Chapter 3:
"Building Your Student Base: A Proven Marketing Strategy"

Chapter 4:
"Lesson Planning, tailoring to an individual's personal needs"

Chapter 5:
"First Contact and Payment Plans (giving you the financial security to build a better life)"

Chapter 6:
"Expanding Your Reach through Workshops and Assemblies"

Chapter 7:
"Budget Control and Accounting Practices"

Chapter 8:
"Mastering the Art of Daily Routine and Student Engagement"

Chapter 14:
"Turning Your Hobby Knowledge into Worldwide Published Books"

The Epilogue:
"Harmony in Entrepreneurship"

**Introduction
: "Profitable Pursuits: Unleashing Your Passion for Financial Freedom"***

In today's fast-paced world, many of us dream of turning our hobbies into a source of income, just as I have successfully done with my passion for drumming. This introduction explores the simple yet well-constructed techniques that have enabled me to transform my love for drumming into a sustainable career as a drum teacher. Through effective self-promotion and the implementation of monthly student payment plans, I not only followed my passion but also created a safety net for myself and my family as a self-employed individual. This pursuit of turning one's hobby into a full-fledged profession offers the allure of being your own boss while reaping the benefits of financial security, making it an attractive and achievable endeavour for those seeking to blend their passion with their livelihood.

This book serves as a comprehensive guide for individuals eager to transform their hobbies into a lucrative source of income and establish financial security for their future. It outlines a step-by-step roadmap for achieving this transformation by drawing inspiration from the remarkable journey I took as drum teacher who effectively monetised my passion for percussion. Through my story, this book demonstrates the key principles that are pivotal in transitioning from hobbyist to successful entrepreneur.

The book is structured in a manner that first delves into the fundamental concept of aligning one's passion with a profitable venture. It emphasises the importance of choosing a hobby that resonates deeply with the individual and can resonate with a broader audience. It encourages readers to reflect on their interests and how these can be turned into a viable business model.

The next part of the book focuses on self-promotion, drawing lessons from my own experience. It delves into the world of marketing, branding, and establishing a digital presence, offering practical advice on how to effectively reach potential customers and clients.

Monthly payment plans, as exemplified by my case, become a cornerstone of financial stability for self-employed individuals. The book provides insights on how to design and implement such plans, ensuring a steady income stream that offers security in an otherwise uncertain entrepreneurial journey.

In essence, this book combines the personal success story I achieved with a structured framework that guides readers through the process of turning their passion into profit. It provides not only inspiration but also concrete strategies, tips, and advice to empower individuals in their quest to be their own boss, enjoy financial security, and ultimately make a living from what they love most. Whether you aspire to become a drum teacher like myself or venture into an entirely different domain, this book equips you with the knowledge and tools to embark on your journey toward turning your hobby into a successful business.

Chapter 1: Teaching as a Passion: Turning Knowledge into Profit

Teaching is a noble and fulfilling profession that, when aligned with your passion, can be the cornerstone of a profitable venture. This chapter will guide you through the process of turning your passion for teaching into a successful self-employed career. We'll highlight the significance of choosing a subject or field that deeply resonates with you and can be appreciated by a broad audience. In addition, we'll encourage you to explore your personal interests and contemplate how they can be transformed into a viable business model within the realm of education and instruction.

The Joy of Teaching

Teaching is a vocation that enables you to share your knowledge, inspire others, and make a meaningful impact. When your passion aligns with the subject matter you teach, it transforms your role from a job into a calling. Whether you're passionate about mathematics, language, art, or any other subject, this chapter will guide you in making the most of your enthusiasm for teaching.

Identifying Your Teaching Niche

As you consider the teaching profession, it's essential to identify the niche that best suits your expertise and passion. What subject or field do you feel most strongly about? What are you knowledgeable and passionate enough to teach effectively? Your niche should align not only with your interests but also with the interests of potential students or learners.

For instance, if you have a passion for history, you could focus on niche areas like ancient civilisations, local history, or a particular historical era that captivates your interest. Your expertise and enthusiasm within your chosen niche will set you apart and draw students to your teaching services.

Recognising Educational Demand

In the realm of teaching, understanding the demand for your subject matter is vital. Research the educational landscape, identify what students or learners are seeking, and find opportunities where your expertise can meet these needs. By addressing gaps in the educational market, you can turn your passion for teaching into a profitable venture.

Reflecting on Your Interests

Your interests and passions are your most valuable assets in the field of teaching. Think deeply about your own hobbies, subjects you excel in, and areas where you have a natural teaching talent. These are the clues that can lead you to discover unique angles within your chosen teaching niche.

For example, if you have a passion for cooking, your teaching niche could revolve around culinary arts. Consider specialised classes in baking, international cuisines, or healthy cooking, aligning your interests with market demand.

Crafting Your Teaching Business Model

Transforming your passion for teaching into a profitable venture involves crafting a viable business model. This includes designing lesson plans, setting pricing structures, and outlining the unique benefits of your teaching services. Your goal is not just to impart knowledge but also to create a financially sustainable income from your teaching passion.

Teaching is a profession that can empower both you and your students, and when approached with genuine enthusiasm, it can also be a rewarding self-employed career. As you embark on this journey, start by reflecting on your interests, the demand in the educational market, and your expertise. Use these insights to construct a successful business model, one that not only fulfils your passion for teaching but also offers the financial security you seek.

Chapter 2: My Journey into becoming self employed : Triumph Over Adversity

My path to becoming a successful drummer and percussionist was not without its share of challenges. Early in my life, I faced the struggles of dyslexia, a condition not widely recognised in those days. Yet, it was music that emerged as my guiding light, opening up a world of creativity that allowed me to transcend the difficulties I encountered in traditional education.

Dyslexia: An Unseen Hurdle

Growing up, I faced academic challenges that were often misattributed to a lack of interest or ability. The true cause of my difficulties, dyslexia, remained undiagnosed. In an era when dyslexia was not widely understood or addressed, I navigated my school years with an unshakeable determination to overcome my academic setbacks.

A Music Teacher's Encouragement

It was during my school years that my journey took a life-altering turn. When my school's music teacher Mr Evans recognised my unwavering passion for music and saw beyond the struggles I faced in the classroom. With a caring and astute eye, the music teacher encouraged me to explore the world of rhythm and beats by trying my hand at drums.

It was a pivotal moment in my life. As I began to learn and play the drums, I discovered an avenue of expression that was liberating. The written shapes of words and letters no longer posed the same obstacles as they did in my academic pursuits. Music provided a new language, one that resonated with me on a profoundly intuitive level.

Drumming as a Forte

With the guidance of my music teacher, I honed my drumming skills and ventured into the world of percussion with unparalleled dedication. The rhythmic patterns and beats became not just a musical pursuit but a means of self-expression and liberation from the constraints of dyslexia. With my improvisation techniques I began to flourish as i delved deeper into the world of drumming.

The Army: A Pivotal Opportunity

After completing my schooling, I embarked on a life-changing journey by joining the army as a professional musician. With my audition for the military band I demonstrated my musical talent, earning me a coveted place among other army musicians. However, my struggle with dyslexia came to the forefront during the educational examination, and I faced a setback. But my musical abilities remained unparalleled, and this was my true strength. Despite the written examination results, I was embraced as an army musician, proving that talent and dedication can outweigh academic challenges.

Life's Toughest Test

Following my service in the army, I transitioned into civilian life, taking on a regular job to support my family. Tragedy struck when my youngest son, Anthony, was diagnosed with a brain tumour and, sadly, passed away at the tender age of two. This was an immeasurable loss for myself and Vanessa, my wife and oldest son Benjamin, one that would forever shape our life's and give me the determination to provide for my family.

In the midst of this heart-wrenching period, I faced the daunting challenge of securing a stable income for my family. It was during these trying times that I decided to turn to what I had learned as a professional drummer and percussionist. Teaching music privately became my calling and the path to both financial stability and the fulfilment of a lifelong passion.

As our business found its groove and brought more smiles to our faces, life surprised us with another blessing—the birth of my new and loving son Christopher Clarke. Welcoming him into our family added a fresh layer of joy and chaos. Amid the daily hustle, we couldn't help but feel Anthony Clarke's presence casting a positive vibe. It's like he's cheering us on from above, giving us the mojo to stick together as a family squad and supercharge our business game. Here's to building success, celebrating diaper changes, and embracing the wild ride of family life!

The greatest fulfilment in life emerges from witnessing the triumphs of those we hold dear. My two sons, Benjamin and Christopher, exemplify this joy through their remarkable achievements. Benjamin's journey as a skilled coder has propelled him to extraordinary success in his chosen field. His family has expanded, welcoming two delightful granddaughters, Ruby and Erin, along with the my daughter-in-law, Samantha who always makes me smile with great banter . Meanwhile, Christopher, the youngest, navigated the challenges to a high level in management in his initial career, eventually transitioning to an entirely new industry during the upheavals of the COVID era. His perseverance and adaptability have led to substantial success, creating a beautiful life alongside his loving wife, Harriet who always keeps me on my toes when playing cards and always pulls me up for not playing corectly lol 😂 . Reflecting on their accomplishments, I find immense satisfaction in knowing that the foundations laid by my self and Vanessa and a successful business have become stepping stones for my family's aspirations, allowing them the freedom to pursue their dreams with the support of devoted parents. The anticipation of more joyous moments, including the prospect of additional grandchildren, fills Vanessa and me with gratitude and pride.

Vanessa, my wife, has been the unwavering bedrock of my journey in building a successful business. In the intricate tapestry of life, support is the thread that binds us, and I am fortunate to have a loving partner who has consistently stood by me, enabling our shared aspirations to materialise. From the early days of our marriage, Vanessa played a pivotal role in constructing the foundations of our household, turning challenges into opportunities for happiness, especially for our sons Benjamin and Christopher. Her selfless commitment to our family saw her sacrificing her own career, epitomising the profound sacrifices made for our collective growth. As we move forward as a united family, Vanessa's support remains an indispensable force, a testament to the irreplaceable role that a special someone can play in helping us achieve our goals. Her enduring presence exemplifies the reciprocal nature of support in our interconnected lives – be there for others, and they, in turn, will be there for you.

My story is a testament to the transformative power of music and the resilience of the human spirit. My journey from struggling with dyslexia and a heart felt loss within the family when I was only so young my self to becoming a celebrated musician and dedicated teacher should be seen as a source of inspiration for those who dare to dream and persist in the face of adversity.

Chapter 3: Building Your Student Base: A Proven Marketing Strategy

Building a thriving student base is crucial to making your self-employed business as a teacher profitable. In this chapter, we'll explore my effective marketing techniques, which have enabled me to attract and retain a steady flow of students. One standout promotion strategy involves setting up stands at local markets, a cost-effective way to engage with potential clients and showcase your teaching expertise.

Market Stand Promotion

One of my tried-and-true methods for student recruitment is setting up stands at local markets.

To get started, you'll want to contact your town's market planners, whose information can typically be found on your council's webpages. Stands usually range from £50 to £100 a day, offering an affordable and high-visibility platform to connect with potential students. The council market managers normally like that this type off stand appears on there streets as it promotes education and I know my market manager was extremely helpful when I started .

Visual Appeal

To make your market stand truly appealing, consider the visual aspect. My technique involves displaying a variety of drums and percussion instruments on a table behind an information desk. This not only catches the eye of passersby but also allows you to speak knowledgeably about your chosen subject due to having visual prompts on you market stand. Plus placing promotion banners on the outside walls of the market stand to attack potential clients to come over and investigate what you have to offer , The brighter the better , I produced my 4 banners In bright yellow with large text

Promotion Flyers / Business Cards

Utilising promotional flyers and business cards, I effectively reach potential clients, highlighting the enticing prospect of a trial lesson to kickstart their musical journey. These materials convey a comprehensive approach to drum lessons, emphasising instruction across diverse styles and aspects. Importantly, the emphasis is on creating an enjoyable learning experience, making each lesson not just educational but also fun. By offering a trial lesson as an initial step, I ensure prospective students can experience firsthand the engaging and versatile nature of my teaching. To take the first step, interested individuals at promotional market stands can take a flyer /business card. If they do not wish to book a trial lesson, then they can visit the website or phone and easily book their trial lesson, providing a seamless pathway to discovering the joy of drumming before committing to a tuition agreement.

"Seeding Success: My Early Days in Direct Marketing"

As I embarked on the journey of teaching and building my own business, I recognised the power of direct marketing in reaching potential students. Armed with a vision and a stack of A5 size flyers, I decided to take matters into my own hands – literally.

In those initial days, I meticulously dropped around 1000 leaflets to homes near me. The response was modest, with just 2 to 3 students showing interest. Yet, this early feedback became the catalyst for my confidence. I understood that the journey of attracting students begins with the first few steps, and I was on my way.

Encouraged by the initial response, I expanded my horizons. Over the next two to three weeks, I ventured further, doing additional mail drops that attracted more students onto my tuition roster. The methodical approach paid off, and I found myself with a growing number of students within the first month and a half of starting my business.

But I didn't stop there. Recognising the diverse avenues available for marketing, I set my sights on the local community newsletter. I secured a paid box ad, strategically placed in full colour, showcasing my teaching business to every home in my home town. This savvy move not only increased my visibility but also brought in a steady stream of new students.

" Local Shops & Community Advertising Boards

In the quest for self-promotion and business expansion, local shops and community advertising boards become valuable allies for the self-employed entrepreneur. These advertising spaces, often available at a reasonable cost or even for free, provide an excellent opportunity to reach out to the immediate community.

Section 1: Utilising Shop Spaces

Most local shops, ranging from grocery stores to cafes, allocate spaces within their premises or on their windows for community advertising. These spaces serve as a direct channel for business owners to connect with potential customers. Whether it's a weekly payable option or a free offering, these opportunities allow entrepreneurs to showcase their products or services to a local audience.

Section 2: The Power of Visual Marketing

Visual marketing materials, such as flyers and business cards, play a crucial role in grabbing the attention of passersby. Having a stack of small flyers in the car or a business card in the wallet ensures that you're always prepared to take advantage of these advertising spaces when you come across them. The ability to spontaneously promote your business fosters a proactive approach to marketing.

Section 3: Supporting the Local Community

Placing your promotional materials in local shops not only benefits your business but also contributes to the overall vibrancy of the community. It's a symbiotic relationship where entrepreneurs gain visibility, and local shops create a dynamic, diverse environment for their customers.

Section 4: The Entrepreneurial Mindset

One of the key points of being self-employed is the perpetual search for ways to promote and build your business. Utilising local shop spaces and community advertising boards exemplifies the entrepreneurial mindset of constant growth and visibility. The more effort and commitment you invest in promoting your business, the greater the benefits you reap.

In conclusion, local shops and community advertising boards serve as valuable avenues for self-employed individuals to promote their businesses. By leveraging these opportunities, entrepreneurs not only enhance their visibility but also actively contribute to the vitality of the local community. Embracing the entrepreneurial spirit of continuous promotion and commitment ensures that your business remains in the public eye, paving the way for sustained growth.

The financial outlay for these marketing efforts proved to be a wise investment. As the flyers landed on doorsteps and the colourful ad graced the pages of the community newsletter or using local storefront promotion, boards or community boards,, my teaching business blossomed. Within a short span, I had a solid foundation of new students within a short tine , a testament to the effectiveness of direct marketing when done thoughtfully and persistently.

While direct mail drops and newsletter ads were integral to my early success, they were not the sole components of my marketing strategy. Market stalls, promotions, and engaging with local schools through workshops and assemblies all played crucial roles. It was a holistic approach that allowed me to carve my path as a self-employed teacher.

In reflecting on those early days, I see them as the seeds I planted, which, with nurturing and strategic planning, grew into a flourishing venture. The lessons learned in direct marketing laid the groundwork for the future, shaping my understanding of reaching students and building a thriving teaching business.

Offer payable cash Trial Lessons

Engage potential clients by offering them a chance to experience you're teaching firsthand.

My approach includes providing trial lessons within that month, initially payable in cash. These introductory sessions give students a taste of your teaching style and what they can gain from your lessons.

Monthly Budget Payment Scheme

After the trial lessons conclude, I would transition my students to a monthly budget payment scheme. The details of this payment plan will be explained further in this book. It's a pivotal step in establishing a consistent income stream while ensuring financial security for your self-employed venture.

Referral System

Turn your students into advocates for your teaching services. I employ a referral system where students who recommend me to others receive one week's worth of fees as an introduction bonus if the new students commit to tuition. This not only motivates your existing students to help promote your business but also establishes a network of satisfied clients working as your marketing team.

School and College Outreach

Don't overlook the opportunity to engage with schools and colleges. Offering free workshops or assemblies can be an effective way to promote your services. By showcasing your expertise and passion, you can capture the interest of students and educational institutions, potentially leading to partnerships or new student enrolments.

Wed-pages promotion platforms
There are many free sights you could join to help promote and get you visibility for your service, I use many music teacher databases webpages which you can upload a writeup and what you offer , local press releases on what you are planning and what you have achieved and what your doing for the local feel good factor, like when I would hold a 2 day fun to drum event in a sports hall away from the neighbours at home when Students would bring there drum kits and they would have two days of drums and drum bands and games , so you can see that the local Press would write a small article on the event, which in turn market's your self employed company

Social Media Presence

In today's digital age, maintaining an active presence on social media is essential. Share your teaching journey, showcase what you're doing in lessons, and keep your audience engaged and informed. It's a valuable way to stay connected with your current students, reach potential clients, and ensure your business remains fresh and up-to-date.

Marketing is a dynamic and essential aspect of your journey as a self-employed teacher or service provider , my strategies offer a mix of offline and online approaches to effectively attract and retain clients . By following these proven techniques, you can build a thriving student base and transform your passion into a profitable career as a private teacher or service provider. Even if you feel you have enough students and do not want any more on your roster. It is still important to continue promoting and marketing the business to keep in the public eye and keep people talking about what you offer and what you have achieved . Remember that teaching is only a small part of running the business when you're not teaching remember that being self-employed you are always promoting and working on ways to build your business and don't forget you only get out of your business what you put in . Work hard enables you to play hard .

Building My First Webpage for Business Success

In the early stages of establishing my business, I recognised the pivotal role a professional website plays in connecting with clients and building credibility. Despite my initial concerns about not being tech-savvy, I discovered an accessible solution – affordable online website templates. These templates provided a user-friendly interface, allowing me to effortlessly insert text and photos into a pre-designed layout tailored to represent my company.

Ease of Use with Website Templates:
Even for those without extensive technical knowledge, the purchase of a website template proved to be a cost-effective and manageable solution. These templates streamlined the process, enabling me to showcase my services and expertise without the need for intricate coding or design skills.

Remember to add visual elements:
Incorporating photos and relevant information into the template was crucial to presenting a professional image. Potential clients were more likely to engage with my services when they could visually grasp the nature of my business through the website.

Keeping Content Fresh:
To ensure my website remained dynamic and informative, I incorporated a basic news section. This section allowed me to provide regular updates, share achievements, and communicate important information with both potential and existing clients. The key was consistency –

updating the news section monthly kept the content current and engaging.

Integration with Social Media:
Recognising the importance of an online presence, I strategically linked my website to various social media platforms, such as Facebook, Instagram, and YouTube. This interconnected web expanded my reach and engaged a wider audience.

Utilize multimedia content:
For a more immersive experience, I utilised a free YouTube channel to share videos of my lessons, updates, and reminders. This not only provided valuable content for existing students but also intrigued potential clients by showcasing the unique aspects of my teaching style.

DIY Approach vs. Hiring a Designer:
Resisting the temptation to hire a website designer, I embraced a DIY approach. While outsourcing may seem convenient, it often results in reliance on the designer for updates, accompanied by recurring hosting fees. Taking control of my website allowed me to manage updates independently, saving both time and money.

Stay in control and on budget:
Managing my own website proved to be a budget-friendly and empowering choice. I had the autonomy to make changes promptly, ensuring that my online presence reflected the current state of my business.

Optimising for Search Engines:
When uploading my website, I seized the opportunity to input relevant keywords. These keywords enhanced the visibility of my website on search engines, attracting potential clients and interested parties searching for services in my niche.

Strategic use of keywords:
Choosing keywords that accurately reflected my services was crucial. This ensured that my website appeared in search results relevant to my offerings.

Strategic Branding:
Maintaining a consistent brand identity, I ensured that my website address visually conveyed the nature of my business. This not only made it memorable but also reinforced the connection between my online presence and the services I offered.

Include website address in social media posts:

Every time I posted on social media, I included my website address. This cross-promotion helped drive traffic to my website and facilitated a seamless transition for those interested in learning more about my services.

In conclusion, building my first webpage proved to be a transformative step in establishing and expanding my business. The accessibility of website templates, combined with strategic content updates and integration with social media, enabled me to create a dynamic online presence. Embracing a DIY approach allowed me to stay in control, optimise for search engines, and reinforce my brand identity. The result was a cost-effective and powerful tool that continues to attract and engage clients, contributing significantly to the success of my business.

After relying on website templates for several years, I found myself exceptionally fortunate when my eldest son, Ben, developed a keen interest in web design and coding. Embracing his newfound passion, Ben took the initiative to build me a personalised, professional-looking website. His expertise in graphic design and coding not only elevated the aesthetic appeal but also provided a unique and tailored online presence. This collaboration allowed for a more visually impactful representation of my business, showcasing the seamless integration of his technical skills with my professional endeavours. While my experience was undoubtedly a stroke of luck, it's worth noting that even individuals without a tech-savvy family member can achieve impressive results using budget template websites available online. I am grateful for the added dimension Ben's skills brought to my online presence, creating a website that stands as a testament to both family collaboration and professional excellence.

Chapter 4 :
Lesson Planning , too an individual's personal needs

In my teaching approach, the focus is always on the student, tailoring each lesson to their unique abilities and preferences. I believe in fostering a comfortable and enjoyable learning environment where the student takes centre stage. Whether working with written music or exploring improvisation styles, I emphasise the importance of adapting to the individual's pace and learning style. Recognising that everyone is different, I ensure that the lesson remains engaging, steering away from excessive academic rigour. For both adults and young children, the goal is not just skill acquisition but also providing a joyful escape. I firmly believe that learning music should be a source of pleasure, offering a break from the stresses of daily life. As the lesson progresses, incorporating play-along tracks in both full-time and half-time speeds adds an element of fun and accomplishment, ensuring the student concludes with a smile. Ultimately, the lesson is about the student's journey, making it an enjoyable and personalised experience.

A common pitfall in teaching is the tendency to overcomplicate lessons, inadvertently shifting the focus from the student to the teacher. By avoiding an exclusive emphasis on graded music exams, I prioritise fostering a genuine passion for music. I firmly believe that pushing students solely towards exams can lead to disinterest and dropout. Instead, I strive to make lessons enjoyable and personally tailored, incorporating techniques and styles that resonate with each student's musical preferences. This approach not only enhances the learning experience but also encourages a deeper and lasting connection with music beyond the confines of formal assessments.Lesson plans can be compiled with the fundamentals (like essential exercises / techniques plus learning how to read music in there instrument which are needed to learning a new skill without affecting the fun element of learning)
Over my time teaching, I have formulated and put together my own Tuition syllabus in the form of a mix of tutor books which are available on Amazon worldwide under the name Glenn R Clarke when searching which I use to teach with in my lessons along with other Music. I see

appropriate to make the Lessons successful for each individual student, but I always finish off the lesson with the student playing along to a musical track at the level they are at the present time leaving the lesson feeling they have achieved.

- Keep the lessons about the student and not about yourself,
- Demonstrate what you are teaching without demolishing the student
- Build the lesson about the students music preference and not the music you prefer
- Keep notes for each student plus also write notes for the student in the tutor book you have recommended for the student to use in the lesson
- Try to keep your lessons one to one and not group lessons to keep the lesson a personal tuition experience for the student.

"Embracing the Virtual Classroom: Revolutionising Music Education through Online Skype Tuition"

As the spectre of Covid loomed over our traditional teaching methods, I saw an opportunity to adapt and innovate. Eager to continue providing quality education to my students, I swiftly transitioned to online lessons, utilising the versatile platform, Skype. Determined to offer an immersive experience, I leveraged multi-camera angles in my studio, a feat made possible by the ingenious software, ManyCam. The Free download lets you use 2 cameras onto one virtual computer screen , a great way to start.

With accessible free downloads and the aid of USB budget webcams and built-in laptop microphones, my students seamlessly integrated their own electric or acoustic drum kits into the virtual lessons using laptops, phones, or iPads. This marked the beginning of a new era in my teaching journey.

Even as the pandemic waned, the online model persisted. Many students, and a growing number still, opted for Skype lessons, or a blend of both virtual and in-studio sessions, depending on the week's demands and travel constraints. This flexibility became a cornerstone of my teaching approach, empowering students to balance their lessons with other weekly commitments.

A pivotal moment in this evolution was my investment in a professional camera switcher., I use a Blackmagic ATEM Mini Camara switcher and Zoom Q8 HDMI Camera's Plus a Behrenger mixer This upgrade allowed me to operate four cameras simultaneously via HDMI, linking them to my computer through a small mixer. Here, I seamlessly connected electronic drums and acoustic drum microphones, creating a rich, immersive learning environment. The camera switcher decoded and transmitted video and audio feeds directly to my students, enhancing the virtual experience.

Moreover, this setup facilitated the integration of written music and audio directly into the lessons, enriching the educational journey. The newfound capability to extend my reach beyond geographical boundaries opened doors to students from all corners of the country and even abroad. It became clear that this blend of technology and teaching was transforming the landscape of music education.

In an effort to streamline communication, I adopted a morning routine of texting each student. This not only served as a reminder but also allowed me to ascertain whether the day's lesson would be conducted in-studio or online. Armed with this information, I could tailor the lesson setup to suit the individual student's needs, ensuring a seamless transition between virtual and physical spaces.

This journey into the realm of online music education has been transformative, not only for me as an educator but for the students who now have the freedom to choose the mode of their lessons. The integration of technology has opened new doors, making music education more accessible and flexible than ever before.

Chapter: 5 First Contact and Payment Plans
(giving you the financial security to build a better life)

There are many a teacher who go one lesson at a time reference cash in hand at the time of the lesson as they just see a lump sum payment at the time which seems impossible to pass down ,

Lots of teachers opt for the convenience of cash payments per lesson, but this method poses challenges to stability and financial predictability. It allows students an easy way to cancel at the last minute without consequences, leading to potential income fluctuations and stress, especially during school holidays or slow periods. To navigate the self-employed teaching journey more smoothly, implement a structured payment system. This should involve monthly budget payment fees, ensuring a consistent income and fostering a commitment from students that goes beyond the immediate lesson. By embracing this approach, you can establish a more secure and stress-free path in your career as a self-employed teacher.

In the world of teaching, the first contact with a new adult student or parent is a crucial step in establishing a successful and mutually beneficial relationship. Whether you're dealing with parents of young learners or adults seeking to expand their knowledge, the initial conversation sets the tone for the entire teaching experience.

As a teacher and business owner, it's essential to communicate clearly about your payment plans. I begin by emphasising the value of the trial lessons, explaining that they serve as an opportunity for the student to sample my teaching style and approach and experience the fun and enjoyment of learning. This initial period is designed to build confidence and trust, laying the foundation for a positive and productive learning journey.

I explain once the trial cash payment lessons have provided a glimpse into the teaching dynamic, I introduce the concept of a budget payment plan. I outline the benefits for both parties—providing consistency and structure for my business while offering flexibility for the students and parents. I highlight the fact that I operate within the framework of school terms, aligning with the academic calendar of the local area.

The term-based approach resonates well with parents and adults alike, as it allows for seamless integration with their holiday plans. The flexibility ensures that lessons continue throughout the term, but not during school breaks, providing a valuable continuity of learning. Importantly, this structure doesn't lock them into a rigid contract reminiscent of a gym membership, allowing for only a full term's notice if they decide to discontinue.

Clarifying expectations is vital, and I stress the importance of timely communication. A full term's notice becomes a standard, mirroring the requirements of various school activities. This policy not only provides me with ample time to fill the vacancy but also allows for the possibility of concluding the notice period earlier if a replacement student is found.

The budget payment plan is presented as a necessity for the smooth operation of my teaching business . Over my 35 years of teaching experience, I've found that this approach not only provides monthly financial stability but also simplifies the payment process for students. With payments spread over a 12-month period, students can plan and manage their finances more effectively, eliminating the need for cash transactions at each lesson.

Contrary to the traditional half hour or hourly cash in hand on the day payment model, the budget plan ensures a steady income, especially during school holidays when uncertainty often prevails. It discourages last-minute cancellations as once on a budget payment, if a parent or adult student cancels a lesson their fee is nonrefundable for that lesson to secure your income. This is a vital aspect to communicate at the start when You have first contact and encourages students to approach their lessons with commitment and consideration for the teacher's time. (don't be put off by having to implement this as it shows your commitment to running a successful and reliable business model and shows you are a reliable teacher and will not let them down reference attendance due to the tuition agreement you have completed with them also the tuition agreement works both ways as your committing to a regular time slot with them each academic term week . The same as any other employed person would have in their own chosen career, a reliable diary time plan and income stream, even when they are unwell and can't attend work.)

In essence, my approach to the first contact and payment plans is rooted in creating a win-win situation. It establishes a transparent framework that benefits both parties—providing financial stability for the teacher and a structured, hassle-free learning experience for the student. Following this plan ensures a successful business venture, allowing teachers to monetise their passion while maintaining a thriving teaching practice. This approach also gives me as a teacher the time within the school holidays time to relax and enjoy time with my family to destress, the things that we must as individuals to make time for yourself and your family , this is a healthy business model,

Additionally, to accommodate those seeking extra lessons outside the regular term schedule, I offer the option for additional sessions on a cash basis. These supplementary lessons are strategically made available periodically during holiday breaks, adding a sense of exclusivity and emphasising the value of my time. By limiting these opportunities to specific intervals, it not only enhances the importance of these sessions but also encourages students, both adults and children, to book in advance. This approach ensures a more organised schedule, allowing students to secure their preferred slots and reinforcing the notion that my time, even during breaks, is a valuable and sought-after resource.

Booking Script: First Contact
You must explain your booking and payment tuition agreement on first contact to avoid awkward situations in the future, don't be scared to say what you expect as it shows professionalism within your business and instils trust with a student or parent that they will be getting the best tuition and service they deserve.

Opening:
. At our lessons, the focus is entirely on creating a fun and tailored experience based on the music you enjoy."

Approach to Reading Music and Exams:
"While we do introduce reading music as a tool to reinforce what we cover in your lessons and aid in home practice, I want to emphasise that there's no pressure to pursue exams unless it aligns with your goals. Even if exams are something you're interested in, I like to split our lessons into two sections: one for exam study and another for enjoyable rhythm studies and playing your favourite styles of music. This helps to keep things engaging and prevents monotony that can arise from continuous exam preparation." Learning to play should be a fun experience and when in lessons with myself this is the main focus not just as an academic study.

Trial Lessons and Payment Information:
"For trial lessons, I recommend starting with a couple, depending on when you begin within the month. Each trial lesson is payable in your currency as a cash payment each trial lesson at £17 - $21 - € 19 per half-hour session at the time of each lesson. After the trial period, we move to a budget payment system to make things convenient for you. This involves multiplying your currency £17 - $ 21 - € 19

by the 40 weeks in the academic year, dividing it into 12 calendar months, resulting in a monthly payment in your currency of
£56 - $70 - €64 . This arrangement doesn't lock you into a yearly contract, but I kindly request a full term's notice if you decide to cancel, similar to the practice at other schools when booking extracurricular activities."

Consistent Lesson Times and Holiday Schedule:
"Your lesson times will remain consistent each week, on the same day and time. This ensures continuity for the best learning experience for both you and me, allowing effective diary planning for the week. as you can understand time slots are very limited and with this in mind if you don't attend or cancel a lesson after moving onto a tuition agreement and after your trial tuition then fees are non refundable as your on a budget payment , but if I have a different slot available that week then it may be possible to move you to that slot but this can not be guaranteed , We don't conduct lessons during school holidays or bank holidays, providing clarity for your holiday planning. The budget payments not only ease your financial planning but also help me concentrate on delivering the best lesson without the distraction of financial considerations."

Summer Lessons:

"I also offer some extra lessons during the summer if students are interested. These are booked on a first-come, first-served basis and are available as one-hour sessions, payable in cash."

Closing:
"It's all about making your learning journey enjoyable and tailored to your musical preferences.

Before embarking on trial lessons, it is imperative to provide students and parents with essential documents that not only fortify the security of your business but also furnish them with a structured guideline for your tuition program. These vital documents serve as a foundation, ensuring clear communication and understanding between both parties. First and foremost, a comprehensive agreement outlining the terms and conditions of the tuition program must be shared, detailing payment schedules, cancellation policies, and any other relevant contractual details.

Providing a comprehensive tuition agreement is paramount for the success of your teaching business. This document serves as a roadmap, clearly outlining your expectations, lesson details, and payment structure. By including trial lesson dates and a transparent payment plan, you establish a foundation of trust with your students or adults. The inclusion of bank stand-in-order information for monthly payments streamlines financial transactions, ensuring a steady income and reducing concerns for both parties. Additionally, furnishing a map with precise directions to your teaching venue enhances the overall experience for your clients, eliminating any confusion. This meticulous approach not only safeguards your income but also affords you the time and peace of mind to focus on providing high-quality lessons, fostering a sustainable and fulfilling career as an independent educator.

Student Tuition Agreement Contract TEMPLATE on the next page

Tuition Agreement

Glenn Clarke: GRC Percussion

Full Address
Teacher . Tel No:
TUITION AGEMENT FORM

Full Name

Address :

Dear — — — —- Ref : <u>booking of Drum Kit</u>
<u>Tuition for :</u>
This is confirmation of the booking of Drum
Tuition
On Thursdays   at 4.30 pm for Half hour's
Tuition
<u>at GRC Tuition Studios , Address :</u>
from 1st of [Date] — — — — — all tuition fees
are to be paid by standing order only, as you
were informed within your initial information by
Glenn Clarke, Tuition is worked out on 38 / 40
weeks tuition per year at £ 17.00 per lesson /
based on tuition within **Hampshire county**
school terms only, divided over 12 months /
paid over 12 months, including bank holidays /
school holidays. £56.00 per Month.

Trial Lesson Dates
———————————————————— at
£17.00 per week payable in cash on each trial
lesson Date

**£ 56.00 per month standing order Total, into
GRC Drum Tuition Account
[Standing Order to be set up and commence
on Date: ————— if you wish to continue
after trial tuition**

*1 full state School terms written notice to cancel
tuition
* If tuition notice is given at the start of the
summer term, your last standing order will be the
1st August.
*Tuition fees are non-refundable unless cancelled
by Glenn Clarke.
*Tuition places with GRC Drum Tuition are at a
premium, which in turn means rules of
cancellation must always apply. Please sign and
date one copy of this agreement and return
ASAP.
*Tuition Fees Non-refundable due to act of God
and Weather conditions making travel unsafe
and closing roads. at GRC Studios , which is
not in the control of GRC.
*At any time within your tuition agreement with
yourself and your teacher you change your
tuition time or day, your tuition written agreement

times changed accordingly, and still abide to the rules of notice and cancellation.

*Overpayments of fees from standing orders are the responsibility of the payee, and standing orders must be cancelled by the payee after any notice lessons & payments are complete, 50% of refund of any overpayments will be deducted for admin.

* in the circumstance of a Government lockdown then lessons will be given by Skype

Please fill your standing order mandate in and hand into your bank / building society your, 1st standing order to be paid on the 1st (Date) plus hand one copy of this form back signed to Glenn Clarke

Full Name_____

Signature ……………..

……………………………………………………

Date …………………….

Glenn R Clarke : Grc Percussion
signature …………………………………….. Date
— —

*Monthly budget payments can be set up by parents, guardians, and adult students using the provided standing order template form provided for online or in-person setup in their respective banks.

GRC Drum & Percussion

Standing Order Mandate

To {Bank} *   {Sort Code}

{Postal Address} *

Please Pay the under noted standing order with effect from 1st { Date }

Signature *   Date   /   /

Please pay the standing order to: -   {BENEFICIARY DETAILS}

Bank Of Scotland	{Sort code}	_____
Edinburgh		
EH11 3XP	{Account Number}	_____

Account Name: GRC Drum & Percussion

Please Pay The Following: -

{Amount}: £ 57.00   {In Words}: Fifty seven pounds

Commencing 1st { Date }   {Due date & frequency} 1st Monthly

To Be Debited from my Account: -   {Remitters Details}

Account Number   A / C no *

Account In The Name Of   *

Signature *   Date   /   /

Please Hand This In To Your Bank [ASAP]

Or set up within your Internet / phone banking
With your 1st Payment due 1st { Date }
glenn@grcpercussion.com

In the world of running a successful tuition business, the key lies in following a meticulous procedure, one that guarantees financial security with monthly assured payments. The foundation of this success is built upon two essential documents, representing the pinnacle of running such an enterprise.

Consider this scenario: dedicating just two days per academic week during term time can yield a substantial monthly income. With 12 students per day, each engaging in half-hour sessions, the total teaching time amounts to six hours per day. Crunching the numbers, this translates to £672 / $846 / €774 per calendar month. Multiply that by two days, and the result is a monthly income of £1344, / $1695 / €1549 accumulating to an impressive £16128 / $20325 / €18593 per year.

Alternatively, for those willing to commit to a more extensive schedule, teaching on all five weekdays (excluding weekends, school holidays, and bank holidays) for 40 weeks in an academic year can be highly rewarding. With 30 hours of teaching per week, accommodating 60 students with half-hour lessons, the monthly income tallies up to £3360 / $4234 / €3873. Over the course of 12 months, this commitment leads to an annual income of £40320 / $50814 / €46489. All of this achieved with a mere 30 hours of work per week, exclusively during school academic terms, and the added benefit of enjoying all school holidays and bank holidays off.

This proven formula extends beyond the private setting. It seamlessly integrates into teaching in private schools, where one-to-one lessons are contracted directly with parents. The business model remains consistent, ensuring stability and ease for both educators and students.

The genius of this approach lies in its consideration for the financial aspects faced by parents and adult students. By implementing a budget-friendly structure, the burden of weekly payments or the risk of lost invoices is eliminated. The introduction of standing orders transforms the payment process into a seamless experience, allowing everyone involved to focus on the true essence of the teaching experience.

"Strategic Sponsorship: Empowering Local Teams Through Efficient Budget Payments"

Sponsoring my local football team involved more than just providing match strips and training tops with my tuition business's logo and website; it showcased the effectiveness of budget payments for fees. By introducing a monthly contribution system for parents instead of periodic lump sums, the financial process became more streamlined. This approach not only alleviated the financial burden on parents but also established a consistent and predictable cash flow for the team administrators. The beauty of this method became evident in the context of the football team sponsorship, where it facilitated the engagement of specialist football trainers and covered various additional costs throughout the season. Its adaptability proves it to be a practical solution in diverse scenarios, simplifying financial transactions and enhancing overall budget management.

Chapter 6 : Expanding Your Reach through Workshops and Assemblies

As a teacher seeking to supplement your income and share your passion, workshops and school assemblies provide an excellent avenue for reaching a broader audience. Beyond one-on-one lessons, the possibilities of offering educational sessions to entire schools or corporate teams can be both rewarding and financially beneficial.

Consider crafting workshops tailored to your expertise, such as my "Rhythm of Life" workshop, which seamlessly blends music and science. The fusion of music with scientific concepts like vibration and density can captivate students and professionals alike. This type of workshop not only showcases your skills but also demonstrates the interdisciplinary nature of your craft.

If public speaking is within your comfort zone, offering workshops during school assemblies or corporate team-building days can be a lucrative venture. Confidence can be built gradually by initially providing shorter, free versions of your workshops to schools. This not only boosts your confidence but also garners referrals and recommendations, acting as valuable promotion for your services.

For those apprehensive about public speaking, starting with smaller, free assemblies and involving a few students can serve as a stepping stone. As confidence grows, transitioning to charged workshops becomes a natural progression.

Promoting your workshops becomes essential, and leveraging online platforms and agencies can significantly expand your reach. Consider creating a digital presence, such as a YouTube channel showcasing snippets of your workshops. Like my YouTube channel, under the name Glenn R Clarke The Crafty Drummer, with demo videos for the "Rhythm of Life" science with music workshop, and my corporate team building ,Beating technology workshop. Both provide potential clients with a glimpse of what you offer.

My "Beating Technology" program, where music becomes a tool for team building. Such initiatives enable teams to collaborate in formulating musical scores using various instruments. The success of this program emphasises the adaptability of workshop concepts to different fields and hobbies.

To further market your services, utilise online agencies that specialise in promoting workshop providers to schools and companies. This not only streamlines the process but also connects you with a broader audience seeking your specific expertise.

In conclusion, workshops and assemblies serve as powerful tools for income supplementation as a self-employed teacher. Leveraging your knowledge and passion, coupled with effective promotion, opens doors to opportunities that extend beyond traditional teaching methods.

Chapter: 7 Budget Control and Accounting Practices

Managing your finances as a self-employed teacher requires a systematic approach to budget control and meticulous accounting practices. Here's a step-by-step guide to help you stay on top of your financial responsibilities.

Monthly Budget Control:
Open a free business bank account

1. On the third of each month, log into your online banking and cross-reference your weekly

tuition diary to confirm each student's monthly budget payment.

2. Mark off payments by ticking or highlighting next to each student's name.

3. Identify any outstanding payments and promptly send a text to the respective adult or parent, notifying them of the missed payment. Encourage them to check with their bank and make a direct transfer, restarting the standing order on the 1st of the following month. Always include your banking information on the text just incase they have mislaid it.

4. Recognise that issues may arise due to banking errors, not the student's fault, and address them promptly.

Personal Compensation and Tax Planning:

1. Once all payments are confirmed in your business account, pay yourself a percentage of the total income into your personal bank account
.

2. Reserve 25% of the monthly fees in the business account for tax purposes at the end of the tax year.

3. After settling the tax bill, consider rewarding yourself with a small bonus from any remaining balance.

Comprehensive Accounting:

1. Include all eligible expenses when completing your accounts for the year.

2. As a self-employed teacher, claim allowances for running costs, including broadband fees, electricity, water percentages, fuel car expenses, insurances, public liability, and key-man insurance (life insurance / critical illness cover)

3. Claim for complimentary hot drinks provided to parents, along with marketing and promotion costs.

4. Include mobile phone and home / landline phone expenses in your claims.

5. Claim a percentage of the amount paid to your spouse or partner if you have one for administration and bookkeeping, ensuring a fair monthly transfer into their account.

6. Keep thorough records of all expenses, retaining and printing receipts for both physical and online purchases.

7. Minimise your yearly tax bill by claiming eligible expenses and deductions accurately. Enter all these expenses into an accounts book/ledger, which is available on Amazon or any other outlet, keep all receipts in a monthly envelope and compile them at the end of that tax year.

Professional Assistance:

1. Consider hiring a local accountant to complete your tax records each year.

2. Pay the necessary fee for their services, knowing that their expertise can help optimise your financial situation.

By adhering to these practices, you'll not only maintain control over your budget but also ensure that your accounting is thorough and compliant, ultimately leading to a more financially stable and rewarding teaching business.

Chapter 8: Title: Mastering the Art of Daily Routine and Student Engagement

In the world of teaching, maintaining a disciplined routine is not just a habit; it's a key to unlocking a day of productivity and ensuring your students receive the attention they deserve. My journey toward a well-structured daily routine has been guided by a simple yet effective strategy – a morning check-in with my students, ensuring they are not only reminded of their lessons but also allowing for dynamic schedule adjustments.

Each day begins with the ritual of reaching out to my students through text messages, a digital roll call that not only sets the tone for the day but also acts as a proactive approach to managing my schedule. As the first rays of sunlight peek through my window, my fingers dance across the keyboard to compose personalised messages for each student, referencing the day's diary.

This routine serves a dual purpose. Firstly, it provides me with a preliminary headcount, allowing me to anticipate attendance, in Studio or via online Skype tuition and to rearrange any vacant slots caused by cancellations. This flexibility is crucial for optimising my schedule, maximising teaching hours, and ensuring a steady flow of lessons throughout the day.

The second and equally significant benefit is the elimination of the "I forgot" excuse. By sending these morning reminders, I empower my students to be accountable for their scheduled lessons. It's a subtle yet effective nudge, gently reminding them of their commitment and helping them stay on track. This proactive communication not only fosters a sense of responsibility among students but also streamlines the overall teaching experience.

In instances where cancellations occur or adjustments are needed, this early check-in becomes invaluable. I can strategically move students to slightly earlier slots, creating a domino effect that not only benefits my schedule but also enhances the overall quality of the learning experience. Students find themselves with more focused, undivided attention during these adjusted sessions, fostering a conducive environment for meaningful engagement.

The key to success in this routine lies in consistency. By making this morning check-in a non-negotiable part of my daily ritual, it has become second nature. It's not just a task to be completed; it's a cornerstone of my teaching practice. The initial effort invested in crafting personalised messages reaps dividends throughout the day, ensuring a smooth and efficient teaching schedule.

In conclusion, the art of a well-structured daily routine is not just about time management; it's about proactive engagement with your students. By embracing the power of morning check-ins and strategic scheduling adjustments, I've not only streamlined my professional life but also empowered my students to take ownership of their learning journey.

- *YOU* Still Get Paid Due To Student Cancellations,

It's imperative for students to remember that in the event of a lesson cancellation by themselves , they remain financially responsible according to the terms of their budget payment plan and the signed tuition agreement contract. As outlined during the initial phone call and reiterated in the contract, lesson fees are still applicable even if a student cancels. This policy, which students agreed to after their trial tuition, ensures a fair commitment to the agreed-upon schedule. However, flexibility exists within the week of cancellation – if a slot becomes available, students may have the opportunity to reschedule, although this cannot be guaranteed. Clear communication and adherence to the terms laid out in the tuition agreement are essential for a smooth and mutually beneficial learning experience.

Chapter 9 : Safeguarding and Professionalism in Private Teaching

Ensuring the safety and well-being of both yourself and your students is paramount when engaging in private teaching. There are crucial checks and policies that, at times, may be overlooked but are indispensable in fostering a secure and professional learning environment.

1. **Criminal Background Check (CRB) or Equivalent:**
Before embarking on private teaching, it is imperative to undergo a thorough criminal background check. This is especially crucial when working with children and vulnerable adults. In many countries, including the UK, this is commonly known as a DBS check. Opting for an enhanced check, even if it incurs a yearly cost of £14 / $17 / €16, expands you're teaching horizons. With a standard check, you're teaching is limited to one designated venue or school. This check is a foundational step to ensure the

safety and suitability of individuals in roles involving frequent interaction with students.

2. **Public Liability Insurance:**
Equally important is safeguarding yourself against unforeseen incidents. Acquiring teachers' public liability insurance provides protection against bodily injury and property damage claims. Imagine a scenario where a student is injured due to a mishap in your teaching space or if any of their possessions get damaged during a lesson. I invest approximately £8 / $10 / €9 per month for my coverage, and I proudly display my public liability certificate in my teaching room or keep a copy in my teaching folder. This not only shields you from potential financial liabilities but also instills confidence and trust in your students.

3. **Building Confidence and Trust:**
Displaying transparency in your commitment to safety and professionalism fosters a sense of confidence and trust among your students. Your adherence to necessary checks and the tangible proof of your insurance coverage communicates a dedication to their well-being, contributing to a positive and secure learning atmosphere.

4. **Tax Deductibility:**
In addition to safety measures, it is essential to be mindful of the financial aspects of your private teaching venture. Keep detailed records of all

payments related to your teaching, as these are tax-deductible expenses. By doing so, you can claim these deductions during the financial tax year, minimising your tax liability and optimising your financial position.

In conclusion, safeguarding oneself and one's students is not only a legal requirement but also a demonstration of professionalism and commitment. The investment in checks, insurance, and financial record-keeping not only ensures compliance but also contributes to a positive and secure educational environment. As you embark on your private teaching journey, remember that prioritising safety and professionalism is a cornerstone of a long-term business venture.

Chapter 10 : Finding the Right Premises Prioritising Your Teaching Diary effectively

Many educators I'm acquainted with have opted for the practice of teaching and conducting lessons at students' and parents' homes. I perceive this as an inefficient use of time within one's schedule, given the additional time spent on travel that could otherwise be utilised for accommodating more students. Teaching in a personal venue, be it at home or in a rented studio, would not only optimise scheduling but also eliminate the added cost and inconvenience of frequent travel. This approach seems more conducive to building a successful teaching business, and I strongly recommend considering it for a more streamlined and cost-effective operation.

When venturing into the world of starting a business, especially one involving acoustic noise like music instruction, the challenge lies in choosing the right space. As a music teacher, I embarked on this journey by considering both practicality and cost-effectiveness.

In the initial stages, mindful of costs, I opted for a budget-friendly approach. I acquired a modest shed for my garden, transforming it into a functional teaching space. Insulating the walls, adding plywood, and investing in quality carpet tiles for sound dampening laid the foundation. Enhancing the door with an additional frame and thick curtains further contributed to effective soundproofing.

For four years, this humble shed served as my teaching sanctuary without any disruptions. The location, at the end of a residential area next to woodlands, played a pivotal role. However, recognising the evolving landscape of music technology, I explored alternatives like silent practice units and headphone systems for instruments, expanding the possibilities beyond traditional setups.

As demand grew, I transitioned to a rented teaching room within a local university. The arrangement not only provided a conducive space but also established valuable connections. Offering scholarship lessons to a couple of university students not only benefited them but also became a strategic marketing move, aligning my services with a reputable institution.

In the subsequent stage of business development, I spearheaded the expansion by strategically recruiting more teachers and diversifying the range of musical instruments offered. To bolster growth, a combination of targeted marketing initiatives and positive word-of-mouth referrals played a pivotal role. As part of this expansion, I crafted a nuanced fee structure, incorporating a monthly budget payment to teachers, complemented by a meticulously drafted self employed contract prepared by an employment lawyer . This contractual safeguard not only shielded me from potential teachers poaching students from my database but also ensured a fair distribution of fees to the teachers. The foundation of this sustainable financial model was laid through a comprehensive tuition agreement contract mutually agreed upon at the commencement of lesson bookings to the Students parents or Adult student plus a Teachers contract which any teacher who stated work for me would need to sigh before

Commencing teaching with myself.

Chapter 11 : Importance of Contracts with Subcontractor Teachers in a Teaching Education Business

In the dynamic world of teaching education, establishing clear and comprehensive contracts with subcontractor teachers is essential for the smooth functioning of your business. The terms and conditions outlined in the contract between my business, GRC Drums & Percussion, and subcontractor teachers play a crucial role in maintaining a harmonious relationship. Let's delve into the significance of each section:

1. The Contractual Foundation

The very existence of a written contract provides a solid foundation for the business relationship. The stipulation that no variation is valid unless approved in writing ensures that both parties are bound by the agreed-upon terms, promoting clarity and preventing misunderstandings.

2. Definitions for Precision

Clearly defined terms such as "Commencement Date," "Curriculum," "Duties," and others eliminate ambiguity. This meticulous approach sets the stage for a shared understanding, minimising the risk of disputes arising from misinterpretation.

3. Performance of Duties

The section outlining the subcontractor's responsibilities, from executing teaching services to participating in additional events, establishes expectations. The subcontractor's exclusive liability to students reinforces accountability, emphasising the importance of their role.

4. Subcontractor's Obligations

This segment outlines the subcontractor's commitments, from maintaining professionalism to adhering to health and safety guidelines. The subcontractor's responsibility to handle complaints promptly ensures a proactive approach to issue resolution.

5. Payment of Fees

The clear terms regarding payment, including the specified fee and payment schedule, create transparency. Providing an option for the subcontractor to receive payments over a 12-

month period demonstrates flexibility and accommodates different preferences.

6. Expenses and Taxation

Agreeing on expenses beforehand and clarifying the subcontractor's responsibility for taxes ensures financial clarity. The option for the subcontractor to nominate a payment structure over 12 months adds a layer of financial convenience.

7. Confidentiality and Intellectual Property

This section protects the business's intellectual property and confidential information. It establishes the boundaries within which the subcontractor can use or disclose information acquired during the contract, safeguarding the business's interests.

8. Termination and Post Termination Restrictions

Clear guidelines for termination, coupled with post-termination restrictions, protect both parties' interests. The non-compete clause ensures that the subcontractor does not engage in activities that could undermine the business's position in the market.

9. Relationship between the Parties

Acknowledging that the contract does not establish an employer-employee relationship reinforces the subcontractor's independent status. This understanding is crucial in the context of legal responsibilities and obligations.

10. Dispute Resolution

Including a mechanism for dispute resolution through arbitration provides a structured and fair process for handling conflicts, reducing the likelihood of prolonged legal battles.

In conclusion, a well-crafted contract is the cornerstone of a successful relationship between a business and its subcontractor teachers. It sets expectations, ensures accountability, and provides a framework for dispute resolution, ultimately fostering a collaborative and productive partnership in the realm of teaching education.

You will find a copy of my complete teacher's Sub contractor contract template Below for your reference.

DATED :

1. **MR G CLARKE t/a GRC DRUMS & PERCUSSION**

2. **[Name :**   **THE SUB-CONTRACTOR]**

TERMS AND CONDITIONS FOR THE SUPPLY OF SERVICES

Mr G Clarke t/a GRC Drums & Percussion
Address :
TERMS and CONDITIONS for the supply of Services

between:

1. **Mr Glenn Clarke trading as GRC Drums &
    Percussion
    Address :
    ("GRC"); and**

2.

    **Name :   {the Sub-
    Contractor}
    Address :**

....
...

Whereas:

1.   GRC is engaged in the business of
supplying private music lessons (in particular
Guitar & Bass Guitar And Drums & Percussion
instruments) to any person who may require such
lessons.

2.   The Sub-Contractor agrees to supply their
services as a Music Teacher specialising in
Acoustic & Electric Guitar & Bass Guitar to GRC.

3.   In reliance of the Sub-Contractors' skill,
knowledge and experience, GRC agrees to
provide Students to the Sub-Contractor, such
Students to remain at all times the contacts of
GRC.

1. **The Contract**
1. No variation or alteration to this Contract shall be valid unless approved in writing and signed by GRC and the Sub-Contractor.

2. **Definitions**
1. In all contracts to which these terms and conditions apply:
2. "Commencement Date" means ***Date :*** "the Contract" means this document evidencing the agreement (or any subsequent document(s) evidencing the agreement) between GRC and the Sub-Contractor for the provision of services by the Sub-Contractor to GRC and all conditions set out in this agreement (or any subsequent agreement as agreed by GRC and the Sub-Contractor);
3. "Curriculum" means the guidance given in GRC's "Guitar / bass note sheets as supplied by GRC or other guidance as approved and notified to the Sub-Contractor by GRC from time to time;
4. "Duties" means the provision of services as a music teacher specialising in drums and percussion by the Sub-Contractor to GRC in accordance with the Contract;
5. "Additional Duties" means any promotional / educational events held by

GRC from time to time notified to the Sub-Contractor by GRC giving not less than 2 weeks' notice of such event

6. "Relevant Territory" means a radius of 10 miles of any of GRC's Studios that are in use at the time of the termination of the Contract or have been used in the 6 months prior to the termination of the Contract;

7. "Students" means those persons requiring private music lessons (in particular Guitar / Bass Guitar instruments) from GRC whom GRC require the Sub-Contractor to teach in accordance with his Duties;

8. "Studios" means GRC's studio at GRC Teaching studios , **Address :** or any other studio that may from time to time be used or acquired by GRC within a 10-mile radius of Sub-Contractor's home address;

9. "Working Weeks" means those weeks that constitute term time based on the County of Hampshire schools' academic year up to a maximum of 40 weeks per annum.

3. **Sub-Contractors' Performance of Duties**
1. The Sub-Contractor shall carry out the Duties of providing music teaching services to Students referred to them by GRC at the Studios during the Working Weeks in accordance with the Contract with effect

from the Commencement Date until terminated in accordance with the Contract.

2. The Sub-Contractor shall make himself available for Additional Duties notified to him from time to time by GRC provided that GRC provides the Sub-Contractor with no less than 2 weeks' notice of the requirement to perform such Additional Duties.

3. The Sub-Contractor shall ensure that all the facts upon which GRC makes its decision to accept the Sub-Contractor's provision of services to GRC are materially correct.

4. The Sub-Contractor shall perform the duties set out in this Contract to the reasonable satisfaction of GRC.

5. The Sub-Contractor will determine the method of work appropriate to the most effective execution of the Duties with reference to the Curriculum. GRC shall not be entitled (and will not seek) to supervise, direct or control the Sub-Contractor in the manner of execution of the Duties save that it shall require the Sub-Contractor to follow the Curriculum.

6. The Sub-Contractor will be exclusively liable to the Students for any claim, loss, damage, cost or expense incurred by the Student or otherwise arising in connection with any act, omission or neglect on the part of the Sub-Contractor in or in connection with the execution of his obligations under this Contract.

7.   The Sub-Contractor shall indemnify and save harmless GRC against any claims, loss, damage, cost, expense, demand or proceeding whatsoever incurred by GRC arising out of or in connection with the execution of, or any failure to execute, his obligations under this Contract.

4.   **Sub-Contractor's Obligations**

The Sub-Contractor agrees on their own part that they shall:

1.   not engage in any conduct detrimental to the interests of GRC or the Students;
2.   execute the Duties and Additional Duties at such times as may be so agreed;
3.   be smartly dressed and wear GRC's merchandise (provided to the Sub-Contractor by GRC on the Commencement Date) at all times whilst representing GRC;
4.   ensure that all Students wear suitable ear protection during all music lessons and comply with any other Health & Safety guidance from time to time in force;
5.   comply with any rules or obligations in force at the Studios where the Duties are being executed;
6.   cancel any appointments with Students with as much notice as possible in the event of the Sub-Contractor not being able to perform the Duties owing to their sickness or other important prior

engagement and re-arrange such appointments wherever possible within 8 weeks of such cancellation occurring and retain records of cancellations and re-arranged appointments;

7. notify GRC immediately that the Sub-Contractor becomes aware that they are unable to attend an appointment with a Student;

8. not cancel any appointment with any Student except in accordance with clause 4.6 of this Contract without the written consent of GRC;

9. notify GRC immediately that the Sub-Contractor becomes aware of any complaint or potential complaint from a Student against them or GRC;

10. retain up to date contact details for all Students;

11. prepare and retain lesson plans and tuition records for all Students and produce such documents to GRC within 5 days' of request;

12. prepare a draft progress report for all Students on a 6 monthly basis to be approved by GRC before providing such report to the Students and ensure that a copy of the final progress report and provided to GRC within 5 days' of request;

13. utilise GRC's headed notepaper for any correspondence with Students and retain copies of any correspondence with all

Students such copies to be provided to GRC within 5 days' of request;

14. be responsible for effecting and maintaining (at their own cost) all relevant insurance including (for the avoidance of doubt but without limitation) public liability insurance in an amount not less than £500,000 per occurrence; and

15. Provide to GRC such evidence of insurance as GRC requires.

5. **Delegation of Duties**

1. The Sub-Contractor shall only delegate their Duties to a music teacher approved by GRC.

2. Such delegation of duties shall only be permitted by GRC in the event of the Sub-Contractor's sickness or otherwise with express written permission of GRC.

17. **Payment of fees**

1. GRC shall pay the Sub-Contractor a fee of £12 per hour for time spent executing the Duties.

2. GRC shall pay the Sub-Contractor a fee to be agreed for the execution of the Additional Duties.

3. GRC shall be solely responsible for the payment of all fees due to the Sub-Contractor in respect of the execution of the Duties.

4.   The Sub-Contractor shall submit to GRC on the first Tuesday in every month:

1.   tax invoices for fees calculated by reference to the time spent executing the Duties and Additional Duties confirming the total number of hours spent by the Sub-Contractor complying with the Duties and Additional Duties for the previous calendar month.

5.   GRC shall make payment of amounts properly invoiced to GRC by the Sub-Contractor on the 13th day of each calendar month or, if this day falls on a weekend or public holiday, the first working day thereafter, such payment to be made by bank transfer to the Sub-Contractors' nominated bank account.

6.   GRC shall be entitled to deduct from any amount due to the Sub-Contractor any amount it is required by law to deduct and shall account for such amounts to the appropriate authorities.

7.   GRC shall be entitled to deduct from any amount due to the Sub-Contractor any amount that has been overpaid in error to the Sub-Contractor.

8.   The Sub-Contractor shall be entitled to nominate (by giving one months' notice to GRC) to receive payment of the fees due to them over a 12-month period rather than receiving payment during the Working

Weeks only. If such nomination is made then fees will be paid by GRC on the same basis outlined in clause 6.5 using the following formula:

Number of hours worked per week x hourly rate {£12.00} x 40 Weeks
Divided into 12 months = Months bank Payment

7. **Expenses**
1. Any expenses incurred by the Sub-Contractor must be expressly agreed by GRC in writing prior to incurring such expenses. In the event of GRC agreeing to pay such expenses, GRC shall be responsible for all reimbursement of such expenses but only to the extent that tax invoices have been received by GRC (see clause 6.4.1 above).

8. **National insurance, income tax, statutory sick pay, and incapacity benefit**
1. The Sub-Contractor shall be responsible for any PAYE, income tax, national insurance contributions and any other taxes and deductions payable in respect of any fees or other income received from GRC. The Sub-Contractor shall indemnify GRC against any such taxes, contributions or deductions as shall from time to time be due from or assessed on GRC.

9. **Liability**

1. GRC does not accept responsibility for or to the Sub-Contractor whether in respect of earnings, pension rights, health, safety or protection from injury or loss of or damage to property while engaged in the execution of the Duties or Additional Duties.

10. **Confidential Information**

1. The Sub-Contractor agrees:

1. that all information furnished to or obtained by the Sub-Contractor in the course of or as a result of executing the Duties or Additional Duties shall be kept confidential by the Sub-Contractor and shall not be used for any purpose other than the execution of the Duties or Additional Duties;

2. that all copyright, trademarks, patents and other intellectual property rights arising from the Duties or Additional Duties shall belong to GRC;

3. to deliver up to GRC at the termination of this Contract for whatever reason all documents and other materials belonging to GRC (and all copies thereof) which are in the possession of the Sub-Contractor including documents and other materials created during the course of the execution of the Duties or Additional Duties; and

4. not at any time to make any copy, abstract, summary or précis of the whole or any part of any document or other material belonging to GRC except when required to

do so in the execution of the Duties or Additional Duties in which event any such item shall belong to GRC.

2.	The provisions of this clause 10 shall not apply to any information which comes into the public domain otherwise than as a result of any unauthorised disclosure by the Sub-Contractor.

11.	**Termination**

1.	Either GRC or the Sub-Contractor may terminate the Contract by giving the other written notice of not less than 10 consecutive Working Weeks' notice for any reason whatsoever.

2.	GRC may terminate the Contract immediately by written notice to the Sub-Contractor in the event that:

1.	the Duties or Additional Duties are not being executed by the Sub-Contractor to the reasonable satisfaction of GRC;

2.	the Sub-Contractor is found guilty by a court of competent jurisdiction of a criminal act that is inconsistent with the continuation of the Contract;

3.	the Sub-Contractor is guilty of unprofessional conduct or any material breach of or non-observance of their obligations under the Contract which is not remedied within 30 days of formal notification thereof; or

4. the Sub-Contractor is guilty of conduct tending to bring itself, themselves, the Student or GRC into disrepute.

3. **Restrictions**

1. Whilst the Sub-Contractor shall be fully entitled to service other contracts during and after the currency of this Contract, where they do not conflict with its obligations hereunder, they agree not to supply their services directly or indirectly whether under a contract of service or for services or in partnership or under a licence or franchise arrangement (including reintroduction by or through another company, partnership, agency or any other organisation) to any Student for whom they have carried out services via GRC during the previous 12 months or to any other person, firm or company to whom he has been introduced by GRC during the previous 12 months.

13. **Post Termination Restrictions**

1. The Sub-Contractor covenants with GRC that they will not in competition with GRC for a period of 12 months immediately following the termination of this Contract for whatever reason, whether on their own behalf or on behalf of any other person, firm, company or organisation and whether as employee, director, principal, agent, consultant or in any other capacity:

1.   entice, solicit or induce (or attempt or assist in doing so) away from GRC to a business or individual which competes (or which once operational will so compete) with those parts of GRC with which they were involved in the 12 months preceding the termination of this Contract, the custom or business of any Student, person, firm or company who during the 12 months preceding the termination of this Contract was a Student, client or customer of GRC and with whom they had material personal contact or dealings on behalf of GRC;

2.   accept or deal with the custom or business of any Student, person, firm or company, who during the 12 months preceding the termination of this Contract was a Student, client or customer of GRC and with whom they had material personal contact or dealings with on behalf of GRC and in relation to those parts of GRC's business with which he was concerned to a material extent during the 12 months preceding the termination of this Contract of a materially similar kind to those provided to the Student, client or customer by GRC during the 12 months preceding the termination of this Contract.

2.   The Sub-Contractor agrees that for the duration of the Contract and for the period set out below after its termination for whatever reason, they will not (except with

prior written consent of GRC) directly or indirectly do or attempt to do the following:

1. for 12 months undertake, carry on or be employed, engaged or interested in any capacity in either any business which is competitive with or similar to the business carried out by GRC within the Relevant Territory or any business an objective or anticipated result of which is to compete with GRC within the Relevant Territory.

14. Relationship between the parties

1. GRC and the Sub-Contractor agree and acknowledge that nothing in this Contract shall constitute the relationship of master and servant or employer and employee or any partnership between GRC and the Sub-Contractor.

15. General

1. The remedies available to GRC under the Contract shall be without prejudice to any other rights, either at common law or under statute, which it may have against the Sub-Contractor.
2. The failure or delay of GRC to enforce or to exercise, at any time or for any period of time, any term of or any right, power or privilege arising pursuant to the Contract does not constitute and shall not be construed as a waiver of such term or right and shall in no way affect its right later to enforce or exercise it.

3.   Each provision of the Contract is severable and distinct from the others. If any such provision is or at any time becomes to any extent invalid, illegal or unenforceable under any enactment or rule of law, it shall to that extent be deemed not to form part of the Contract but (except to that extent in the case of that provision) it and all other provisions of the Contract shall continue in full force and effect and their validity, legality and enforceability shall not be thereby affected or impaired.

4.   Clause headings are purely for ease of reference and do not form part of or affect the interpretation of the Contract.

5.   The construction, validity and performance of the Contract is governed by the law of England and the parties accept the jurisdiction of the English courts.

6.   Any dispute between GRC and the Sub-Contractor relating to this Contract shall be referred with the agreement of both parties to an arbitrator appointed by the President of the Law Society ('the Arbitrator') and the decision of the Arbitrator in relation to the dispute shall be binding on the parties.

Signed   .... Date
For and on behalf of GRC

Sub Contractor Name :   Date of Birth:

Signed   Date

Facing the prospect of a larger premises, the challenge was the potential exorbitant costs associated with renting commercial spaces. A creative solution emerged when I approached local storage companies. This unconventional move resulted in securing multiple units at a fraction of the cost of a standalone venue. The added benefit included all-inclusive utilities, 24-hour access, and the flexibility to manage the space efficiently.

In hindsight, my journey emphasised two key strategies for aspiring educators or business owners:

1. Start Small: Consider beginning with a modest shed or similar space in your immediate surroundings if teaching in the house is not feasible. This cost-effective approach allows for organic growth.

2. Leverage Existing Resources: Forge connections with universities or colleges to explore renting teaching facilities. This not only provides a professional setting but also establishes a connection with an academic institution.

3. Explore Unconventional Spaces: Investigate local storage companies or unconventional venues that offer cost-effective options for expanding your business premises.

Avoid overpaying for unnecessary features and prioritise practicality.

In the realm of establishing a teaching business, the journey is as much about resourcefulness as it is about passion for the craft.

Chapter 12 : Home Teaching
** Information on Soundproofing Your Garden Shed / outbuilding **

Creating a quiet oasis in your garden shed requires careful consideration and strategic steps to keep unwanted noise at bay. The key to effective soundproofing lies in addressing different areas of your shed / outbuilding , from the walls to the windows, floors, and doors.

Step 1: Insulation

Insulating for Serenity

Begin your soundproofing journey by focusing on insulation. This critical step will significantly reduce the transmission of sound through your shed's walls. The right insulation material creates an additional barrier that absorbs sound, preventing it from escaping. Here are some insulation options to consider:

Spray Foam Insulation

Spray foam insulation is a versatile choice that effectively covers ceilings and walls. Its ability to fill tight cracks and crevices ensures comprehensive coverage. Look for DIY spray foam products available online or at local hardware stores.

Fiberglass Insulation

For supplemental insulation and increased sound tightness, layer standard fibreglass rock-wall insulation inside the wall panels. Exercise caution, as fibreglass material can cause itching upon contact with the skin. Ensure you wear proper safety gear when handling fibreglass, available at hardware stores . Then use waterproof plaster boards sheets or chipboard sheets tacked onto the shed wall on-top off the insulation panel's.

*Mass-Loaded Vinyl or Carpet Tiles

Known for its cost-effectiveness and efficiency, mass-loaded vinyl or carpet Tiles is an excellent option for soundproofing shed walls. Installation is straightforward, involving measuring, cutting, and simple application to the shed's walls.

Step 2: Soundproofing Windows

Windows: Gateways for Sound

Windows are common avenues for sound waves to travel through, compromising the soundproofing of your studio shed. Address this vulnerability by soundproofing your shed's / outbuildings windows to minimise both incoming and outgoing noise. Consider using soundproof window inserts for an affordable and easy installation process.

Step 3: Soundproofing Floors

Silencing the Ground Beneath

To prevent sound from traveling through the floors, invest in Soundproof Floor Underlayment. This cost-effective solution can be applied to the shed's floor, providing a barrier against sound transmission. Seal the corners between the walls and the floor before installing soundproof flooring to fortify the defence against sound leakage.

Step 4: Soundproofing Doors

Guarding Against Sound Infiltration

Enhance the soundproofing of your shed's doors economically using weather stripping for the door frame and door sweeps for the bottom. Additionally, employ acoustical caulking under the door sill and install an exterior door sill plate on top to fortify the defence against sound traveling in and out through the door.

By following these steps, you'll transform your garden shed into a tranquil retreat, shielding it from the intrusions of external noise and preserving the peace within.

Chapter 13 :
A Musical Beginning :The 1st cash payable Trial Lessons , (Keeping your Students not loosing them)

The fist encounter with new students starts with a selection off cash payable trial lessons, depending at what point off that calendar month they would start dictates how many weeks they will have weekly trial cash lessons until they would commit to tuition agreement contract with my self

The 1st trial Lesson with a beginner student Adult or Child

With a warm smile, I welcome my new student, whether they are an eager adult or a curious child taking their first steps into the world of drumming. Setting the stage for a positive learning experience, I begin by asking them the simple yet crucial question: "What inspired you to explore the world of drumming?"

As they share their motivations, I emphasise that the key to success in learning any new skill is finding joy and having fun along the way. It's not just about hitting the right beats; it's about enjoying the journey of discovery.

Moving into the practical side of things, I introduce the very basics of drumming by addressing the fundamental element of holding drumsticks correctly. This initial step sets the foundation for a solid technique, ensuring that the student is comfortable and ready to dive into the rhythmic world of drums.

Next, we explore the art of striking the drum. I guide them through the proper technique, highlighting the importance of control and precision. This hands-on approach not only establishes a connection between the student and the instrument but also builds their confidence as they produce their first beats.

To make the learning experience even more enjoyable, I introduce a simple drum rhythm. We start with a slow tempo, allowing the student to grasp the basic pattern without feeling overwhelmed. The magic happens when they play along with a drum-less backing track. This strategic choice eliminates the pressure of keeping up with a full backing track , making the first lesson a comfortable and empowering experience.

Even if we need to adjust the rhythm to half time, the focus remains on building the student's confidence. The absence of a complex percussion arrangement in the backing track ensures that the adapted rhythm blends seamlessly, offering a sense of accomplishment without sounding out of place.

Throughout this initial lesson, I steer clear of written music. The goal is to keep things simple and engaging, avoiding potential overwhelm. By the end of the session, the student leaves with a tangible achievement and a newfound excitement for their drumming journey.

Remember, the key is to nurture their interest and enjoyment. This approach ensures that the door to the world of drumming remains wide open, inviting them to return for more rhythmic adventures.

: Nurturing Progress in Trial Lessons

As the second encounter with the new student unfolds, the focus remains on tailoring lessons to their individual abilities. Resist the temptation to overextend, ensuring each lesson is a step forward in their musical journey without overwhelming them. Emphasise their growth and enjoyment rather than showcasing you're teaching prowess.

Introducing basic notation reading becomes a subtle yet pivotal aspect of the lesson plan. This addition shouldn't dominate the allotted time but should serve as a tool for the student. Help them understand that written notation is a guide, a reference for their independent practice at home. This approach transforms the learning experience into a practical and enjoyable activity, particularly when playing along with backing tracks, injecting an element of fun and stress relief for both adults and children.

As lessons progress through the agreed weekly trial period, gradually incorporate more advanced music-reading skills and fundamental techniques. The key is to maintain a balance, keeping the lessons engaging and relevant while instilling a sense of accomplishment. This ensures that the transition into a tuition agreement is a natural progression, enticing the student with the prospect of further growth and musical exploration.

Your ultimate goal during this trial phase is to encourage the student to commit to a tuition agreement with you. This commitment not only provides a stable foundation for your business but also allows you to delve deeper into enhancing the learning experience without concerns about timely payments. Make sure to communicate the notice period clearly, fostering a sense of transparency and understanding.

Remember, each student is a vital piece of the puzzle contributing to the growth of your business. Building a structured and enjoyable lesson plan, focusing on individual progress, and maintaining a balance between education and enjoyment ensures that these trial lessons lay the groundwork for lasting musical connections. Each note played becomes a testament to the bond formed, setting the stage for years of shared musical exploration.

Personal reminders to one's self "
- keep your weekly lessons achievable
- Don't be tempted to try and bring over complicated techniques and studies you may be doing yourself in your own practice (this can sometimes be tempting if you are actively studying this your self and excited about what your doing) keep the lessons about the student.
- This may sound robotic but I have had many a student come to me from other

teachers who have said the reason for leaving lessons with there old teacher was due to the teacher over complicating or always demoralising the student with the teacher over playing and not demonstrating the lesson to a standard the student can achieve.

- If a student wishes study towards an instrumental exam , break the lesson into 2 half's , study exam for first half then move on to working on improvisation / rhythm or melody reading playing along to tracks or playing along to mixed instruments if you can play other instruments. Always finish the lesson on a high.

- Give your lessons continuity, don't bounce around different subject matters simply because you have come across something what interests you in between when you taught the student the week before, this will confuse a student specially if they've been practising to the lesson set the week beforehand.

- Try not to get frustrated with the student. If you feel they are not Moving forward as quick as you think they should be, it's very easy to overcomplicate a lesson due to the standard you are yourself as a teacher, the lesson should be treated like stepping stones ,one step at a time and as long as the student feels they are moving forward and most importantly, enjoying the experience, they will wish to continue on the journey and spending time each week, attending your lessons and enjoying the subject, remember not all students will go on to do this as a career, but mostly do this as an enjoyable hobby. With this in mind keep your lessons enjoyable and achievable and you will have a very profitable and rewarding career as a self employed teacher.

Acknowledgement from one of my students : Craig Hickson : Airline Training Captain

By the end of the trail lesson you will be able to name all the drums, read music and play along to your favourite track!". Really I thought? I had no prior knowledge or experience of drumming and thought this would be a challenge too great for Glenn. He didn't know I had dyslexia and that I had always found lessons tough. In fact I am not good with learning at all, I had always felt small and embarrassed in a classroom environment.

Little did I know at the time that my music teacher, a drumming virtuoso, and I had a lot in common. We both initially struggled to find the passion and drive to succeed. We both found our way in the Military; Glenn in the Army and me in the Royal Navy. As teachers we both understand the need to set the right learning environment, the correct tone where learning can take place in a none threatening place, allowing the trainee to grow. In fact, I stole his phase and say to all the pilots I train "This is going to be fun!"

This book is a moving, candid and eloquent account of how we can all succeed despite significant set backs when we have passion and the love and support from our families.

From a loyal and grateful student. Glenn, thanks for inspiring me, thanks for being patient and most importantly thanks for making my Friday afternoons a blast!

Craig Hickson. Airline Training Captain

Chapter 14 : Turning Your Hobby Knowledge into Worldwide Published Books

Turning your vast knowledge from your beloved hobby into self-published books available worldwide has never been easier, and it can be a rewarding endeavour both intellectually and financially. This chapter will guide you through the steps to share your expertise with a global audience through Amazon's online publishing platform.

Step 1: Compile Your Teaching Material

Start by organising the wealth of teaching material you've accumulated during your journey in your hobby. Gather your notes, lesson plans, and any written content you've created for your students. This will be the foundation for your self-published books.

Step 2: Create a Comprehensive Document

Combine you're teaching material into a single PDF document. Include text, written music, and any other relevant content that you want to share. Ensure that your document is well-organised and easy to follow, as this will enhance the learning experience for your readers.

Step 3: Utilise Amazon's Online Publishing Tools

Take advantage of Amazon's user-friendly online publishing tools. Sign up for a free account on

Amazon's Kindle Direct Publishing (KDP) platform. This platform allows you to publish your work in both digital and paperback formats.

Step 4: Design Your Book Cover

Craft an engaging book cover using Amazon's cover design tools. A visually appealing cover can significantly impact a reader's decision to explore your book. Make sure it reflects the essence of your hobby and the knowledge you're sharing.

Step 5: Set Your Price

Decide on a reasonable price for your book, taking into account Amazon's printing and distribution costs. Remember that Amazon handles the printing, packaging, and shipping, and you only pay for these services when a copy of your book is sold.

Step 6: Global Distribution with Amazon

One of the significant advantages of using Amazon is its global reach. Your book will be available for purchase worldwide, and Amazon will handle the logistics of printing and shipping to customers in different countries and currencies.

Step 7: Earn Royalties and Track Performance

Sit back and watch as your royalties accumulate. Amazon pays you on a monthly basis, providing a transparent record of your book sales and performance through their online dashboard.

Step 8: Share and Connect

Promote your self-published books through your existing networks and social media. Encourage readers to leave reviews, and engage with your audience to build a community around your expertise.

In conclusion, transforming your hobby knowledge into self-published books on Amazon is a straightforward process that allows you to reach a global audience without the need for upfront costs or print runs. Embrace the opportunity to share your passion with the world and enjoy the rewards that come with it.

***Books I Have Written for Teaching Music

When searching books I have written , a savvy approach is to simply search "Glenn R Clarke" on Amazon, but exercise caution as other sellers might inflate prices. To secure these valuable resources at a more realistic and affordable rate, navigate down the listing and include the specific book title in your search. By doing so, you'll ensure a fair deal and gain access to my books without breaking the bank.

Discover the rhythm of learning with two essential tuition books I have written and I use in my lessons, both available worldwide on Amazon.
The first, "The AtoZ Of Drumming Tutor Book: The Right Route For You," is a comprehensive drum kit tutor enriched with MP3s featuring masters of time and 10 play-along charts spanning various styles. From rock to jazz, this book caters to beginners and advanced players alike, offering flexibility for personal improvisation.
The second "The A to Z of Glockenspiel & Xylophone: The Right Route For You," serves beginners and intermediate players, focusing on key signatures, charts, and scales for glockenspiel and xylophone. Clarke's note board charts and shadowed key signatures provide a user-friendly experience, aiding in sight reading and filling a long-standing gap in glockenspiel tutor literature. Search Glenn R Clarke on Amazon to find these invaluable resources at realistic prices, avoiding inflated costs from other sellers.

Glenn R Clarke's Book Collection available on Amazon worldwide : Search Glenn R Clarke on Amazon

1. **The AtoZ Of Drumming Tutor Book: The Right Route For You**
   - Drum Kit Full Tutor book with MP3s
   - 10 play-along Charts covering various styles
   - Suitable for total beginners to advanced players

2. **The A to Z of Glockenspiel & Xylophone: The Right Route For You**
   - For total beginners and intermediate players
   - Key signatures, charts, scales, and note board charts
   - Useful for sight reading preparation for exams and auditions

3. **Build A Study Flip Book For The Drum Kit: Your Essential Sight Reading Book**
   - Essential sight-reading book for drummers

4. **The Stick Bag Buddy: Your Essential Band Practice & Pre Gig Warm Up Book**
   - Band practice and pre-gig warm-up exercises

5. **Christmas Celebrations: For Flute, Piano Keyboard, Recorder, Glockenspiel, Xylophone, Un-Tuned Percussion**
   - Christmas music ensemble for various instruments

6. **DrumLine: 3 x Achievable Original Compositions to Highlight your Un-Tuned Drum-line**
   - Three achievable original compositions for drum-line

7. **FluteTastic: 10 Easy Duets Only Using G-A-B-C**
   - Ten easy flute duets using G-A-B-C

8. **GlockTastic: 10 Very easy Duets for Glockenspiel or Xylophone**
   - Ten very easy duets for glockenspiel or xylophone

9. **Holidays R Coming : Christmas: for Flute Keyboard Recorder Glockenspiel Xylophone Un-Tuned Percussion**
   - Christmas music ensemble for various instruments

10. **Masters of Time: For Drum Kit: with 10 Original Tracks**
    - Ten original tracks covering various styles

11. **RecorderTastic: 10 Very Easy Duets For Recorders**
    - Ten very easy recorder duets

12. **Rhythm Clapping book 1 With Crotchets: Rhythm Clapping with Crotchets**
    - Rhythm clapping exercises with crotchets

13. **Rhythm Clapping book 2 Crotchets & Quavers: Crotchets & Quavers for The Classroom Book**
    - Rhythm clapping exercises with crotchets and quavers

14. **The Main Event book 1 - A selection Of Percussion Ensembles in C Major**
    - Percussion ensembles in C Major for elementary and intermediate players

15. **The Main Event Book 2: 5 Percussion Ensembles in C Major Tuned & Un-Tuned**
    - Five percussion ensembles for tuned and un-tuned instruments

16. **The Main Event Book 3 Percussion Ensembles: 3 Un-Tuned Percussion Ensembles**
    - Three un-tuned percussion ensembles

17. **The Session Classroom Music Performance Pack**
    - School solo or full band performance pack
    - Exam practical performance, improvisation exercises, metronome click training

18. **The Session For Bb Trumpet, Tenor Saxophone**
    - Ultimate play-along & band parts for Bb Trumpet, Tenor Saxophone, & Bb Clarinet

- Includes full parts for Piano, Bass, Guitar, Drums & MP3 play-along tracks

19. **The Session For Eb Alto Saxophone With MP3s**
   - Ultimate play-along & band parts for Eb Alto Saxophone
   - 10 original modern tracks and full band parts

20. **The Session For Flute with MP3s**
   - Ultimate play-along & band parts for flute
   - 10 original modern tracks and full band parts

21. **The Session For Vibraphone & Xylophone with MP3s**
   - Ultimate modern play-along & band music set for vibraphone & xylophone

22. **Timothy Crotchet & The Percussionists Tutor Book for Classroom**
   - Tutor book for classroom percussion instruction

23. **Timothy Crotchet & The Percussionists Story Time Book**
   - Story time book featuring Timothy Crotchet and percussionists

The Epilogue : "Harmony in Entrepreneurship"

As the epilogue unfolds, it resonates with the rhythmic beats of success, echoing the lessons learned from the teaching journey recounted within these pages. The journey, much like the art of drumming itself, is a dance of dedication, rhythm, and passion.

In the pursuit of turning your hobby into financial security, consider the symphony created by aligning passion with practicality. Like a well-tuned drum set, a successful business requires harmony between what you love and what the market demands. It's not merely about hitting the right notes; it's about orchestrating a melody that resonates with both your soul and your audience.

Mastering the art of self-promotion is akin to a drummer showcasing their skills on a grand stage. Embrace the spotlight, share your story, and let your passion reverberate. Social media, networking, and consistent branding become your drumsticks, playing the tune that captivates your audience and leaves an indelible mark.

In the rhythm of financial stability, set the beat with prudent strategies. Monthly payment plans are the metronome that keeps your cash flow steady. Just as a drummer maintains tempo, these financial plans provide a steady rhythm for your business, ensuring that you navigate the highs and lows with grace.

To all the readers, dreamers, and doers, remember this: Your pursuit is not just about turning passion into profit; it's about crafting a life symphony where every beat, every note, contributes to a fulfilling livelihood. The drumming journey shared here is more than inspiration; it's a roadmap for forging your own path, hitting every beat with confidence, and transforming your dreams into a thriving reality.

As the final notes of this book resound, here's to you — the entrepreneur, the artist, the seeker of both passion and financial security. May your endeavours be a crescendo of joy, success, and the sweet satisfaction of doing what you love. Cheers to your journey, and may it be filled with the harmony of turning passion into lasting prosperity.

Glenn R Clarke

instagram : grc_glenn.clarke
Amazon Book Sales : Search Glenn R Clarke

Glenn R Clarke : Professional Drum and Tuned Percussion Teacher and Author ,Tutor books and Percussion ensembles / Classroom music : Amazon worldwide. private and School / Universty instrumental and classroom music teacher. Glenn Clarke's GRC Drum Kit Students continue to hit on the right beat with past and present students going on to work with such bands and artists Girls Aloud , Eminem , Will Smith , Natasha Bedingfield , Sway, Il Divo Glenn R Clarke ,Director of GRC Percussion runs his Private one to one tuition studios from Winchester. GRC Percussion offers

One To One tuition for the drum kit and tuned percussion, for all ages and standards with a more personalised approach.

Tuition is given in all aspects and styles, from modern to classical with students choosing they're own personalised tuition direction. Tuition combines practical musicianship and reading skills incorporated into improvisation training. All students have the opportunity to undertake professional recognised examinations to obtain relative qualifications, GRC Percussion holds a 100% pass rate with all students which have entered into such exams: please note this is optional with no presser given to study such exams. Success goes to strength to strength. As well as tuition Glenn hosts celebrity workshops with such international drummers as Chad Smith RHCP , Dennis Chambers :Santana , Gregg Bissonett : Toto : Steve White : Paul Weller.

Glenn R Clarke

Printed in Great Britain
by Amazon